VIVA LA DIFFERENCE

Viva la Difference

POETRY INSPIRED BY THE PAINTING OF

Peter Saul

OFF THE PARK PRESS :: NEW YORK, NEW YORK

Cover image: *Viva la Difference,* 2008
Acrylic on canvas by Peter Saul,
(American, born 1934)
Painting, 72 x 72 inches
Courtesy of David Nolan Gallery,
New York, New York

Book design by Shari DeGraw

To contact the press, please write

OFF THE PARK PRESS
73 FIFTH AVENUE, 8B
NEW YORK, NEW YORK 10003

ISBN 978-0-9791495-1-1

Off The Park Press books
are distributed by SPD

Small Press Distribution
1341 Seventh Street
Berkeley, California 94710
1-800-869-7553
orders@spdbooks.org www.spdbooks.org

Printed on acid-free paper in
the United States of America.

CONTENTS

An artist never says no.

PETER SAUL

INTRODUCTION

Peter Saul's *Viva la Difference* is the second in a series of anthologies devoted to the work of a single artist. The first one was *New Smoke* (2008), which took the paintings of Neo Rauch as the starting point. The project is straightforward. Every few weeks, a group of poets meet to discuss their poems, as well as subjects, methods, anything having to do with putting words on a page. The idea of writing an ekphrastic poem came up during a discussion about whether or not there were figural paintings where description would not suffice. The work would be the opposite of Edward Hopper's paintings and Joseph Cornell's shadow boxes, which have been the subject of many poems. It is as if they are already poems waiting to be turned into words. Our intention was different; we wanted something that resisted being colonized by language, something that could not be encapsulated. Our intention was not to be an impressionist or to tell a story. Those are well-known solutions, and, frankly, we wanted something else.

All of us go to lots of exhibitions. We decided to limit ourselves to the work of a contemporary artist, someone whose work we all saw and liked. After *New Smoke* was published, we decided to continue the project, as well as invite other writers to contribute a poem about the work we decided was the focus of the next anthology. It was very easy to agree upon Peter Saul's *Viva la Difference* because all of us knew that writing about it would be a challenge. The number of people who we invited and who eventually told us they couldn't do it only confirmed our suspicions.

If there are two imaginations making an effort, that of the artist who made the painting, and that of the poet writing a response, we reasoned that we wanted to choose a work in which the imagination of the artist (the other) could not be accessed, reduced, or explained. A work that might, in effect, defeat any attempt to respond in words.

SUSAN BERGER-JONES

The Princess Constance Summer Delivers
Her Lines to No One in Particular

Most of my performances have not seen the light of day but I'm
   pretty sure they are all for public consumption.

After all, I am a person too.

Usually I prefer to remain a true professional. One has to draw
   the line somewhere.

Don't get me wrong, the entertainment keeps everyone in shape,
   but some of the talent scouts have questioned my
   commitment.

I've declined to give interviews.

The Palace's hallways are often too precious to be used even after
   hours which are usually later than one would think.

While what I do may not be high art, obviously, some of it can be
   very creative.

I am a true connoisseur and the only foot fetish left in Pittsburgh.

Mr. Harry Vanderbilt the Third of Queens, New York knows me
   personally.

I have been painted by Madame Pompidou.

Not that I don't love the work but I am surrounded by golden
platters of fried eggs and greasy guinea hen. So throw me
a raspberry every once in a while.

A wise old woman once told me: If you aren't doing it in your
private life then you shouldn't be doing it on the job.

Sometimes I have to take a seat in the Inflatable Bar & Grille.

I sail off with the illegitimate daughters & sons of the Empire.

You say that my head is a stale moon filled with lovely scatter?

I clutch a lock of Lena Wertmuller's hair.

The desert smells like a working man's shirt.

I fall in love with time.

TODD COLBY

Talking With Dead People

He said he could talk with dead people on the phone
and there was no explanation. The dead people on the other end
were heard explaining things to him about
what it felt like to talk on the telephone when you are dead
and what sort of food they ate and TV shows they watched
and what they did in their free time (surfed the net)
and that sort of stuff. They brought in sound technicians with
their mobile labs in big trucks and found that the voices on the phone
were easily matchable with tapes of the dead people talking.
Everyone got totally freaked out by that. Whenever they saw
him on the phone they hoped he was not calling them
or that he would say "hey I'm talking to you on the phone."
It created a hostile environment in the neighborhood
with people all edgy and anticipating some horrifying
revelation that they were just walking around, though dead.
Everyone was also a little worried about what they might
reveal to someone on the telephone if they were dead.
He got a radio show out of the deal and people listened
in record numbers in 2009. He currently lives alone
in Cobble Hill Brooklyn. You can see him with his cell phone
walking down Warren Street talking in a loud theatrical voice,
which is the way he said the dead like to be addressed:
loud and theatrically.

LORRAINE DORAN

The Whole Is Greater

If you were the air you'd be blue and shaped like
    clouds
        shaped like birds
            & I'd forget the science
of how one makes the storm &
           one is a dark balloon
that warns of its coming.   Before I knew
            their true names
or could tell fair weather
        from stratus
          from column rain
I was another animal
      the grass grew under
in the sun's uneven heating
        of the surface
          of the earth.
Now these walls hold the sky & the birds
    become planes
        sharp-nosed & hovering
above their targets.
        Your colors fade into each other
eyes recede
    & limbs. If all of my animals were armless

they could not escape

        or touch me back

              but with the open

wound of the mouth.

        And there would be no rain.

And I will call them

    duckclouds

       & you

         my demented horse

because I see in you

     a beautiful symmetry.

JUDSON EVANS

Kinderschema

Peter Saul, *Viva la Difference* (2008)

If I could comb myself out of my hair
I'd be airbrushed swish, I'd be home schooled
dereliction, rather than rashers of repo sweets.
All my dashed darlings in their crushed plumage
of blue albumin come crumbling back
as you mumble me in that pedagogy
and I'm all arc of trump, all aureoles
at rims of teacups spinning on dowels.

Or mounding volcanically under the shallows
of your touch, its mismatched subtitles.
My body made perfect in both hands by conch pearl
of soap dish.

Allow me to apply myself like a thousand
funnels to a downpour
of honey. Thus amped and obviated,
I can't shower during holy week for several unrelated
reasons. This is my opening
sale, I'm opening, I'm sailing...

I pick my rain barrel brain over
the lower expectations of curved space,
repeating dismemberment 101.

That keeps me davening, keeps me dwindling down
to a dervish and a half, as my declines stay advances.
I inaugurate and issue handouts of my
sprouting every which way, noodling
rhizomes, corals never breeching
the surface of your cocktail.

EILEEN B. HENNESSY

Explorer's Report

In one such ceremony, a large smiling man
wrapped his arm around a hot pink blob
spiky with pink and black breasts and topped
with straggly yellow rope hairs. Sacrifices
were offered: pink and blue drinks,
bits of fruit, a thin roll on a plate. The shiny
red altar cloth fell in folds to the floor.
Blue clouds snailed in formation across the sky.

JENNIFER HAYASHIDA

On Peter Saul (Laughter)

"It had never occurred to me that viewers would want less to look at."
PETER SAUL[1]

Call me a crackpot in pajamas: I sit on a stump called painting and watch a parade of immodest thinkers march by. They send each other pictures in a can and their pictures have no problems. They reap rewards for their guaranteed techniques.

I look for the racist and sexist ones. Collect an abundance of private parts, lips to tips and teets to teeth, scour museums of calm technical problems, take away the spectators' upper hand when they want different ways to paint a certain white.

Minimalism takes painting away and gives it back like a transcript of silence. Give me paintings like photos of brains blown out, more than just a tangle of arms and legs. Don't give me a C for this painting: I'll be drafted.

There is no woman here, only assorted pieces of anatomy, slick like hot dogs or wet balloons. Like sex between celebrities in a heavy gilded frame. Sometimes a hot dog can be more delicious than the beef it comes from. We need a bit of harm for our own good.

1 Saul Ostrow, "Peter Saul," *BOMB* 104, Summer 2008.

BONI JOI

Viva la Choice

after "Housekeeping" by Lucie Brock-Broido

After the mad-dog of it all, the terrible monologue
of nice, caricatured, relentless am I now to speak

you through a season of conversations moved to the trash
am I to hire a hookworm to dig around the backrooms

of effed-up Greek mortals, whip up martinis of
myself, a soft structure painted up like a

Chinatown dragon. When I think of love I think
of the corner bar. And all those years I had to love

my hands, even though I have no hands.
As the clientele loiter around the piers dressed in

brights, I sit here and pose as your main
squeeze and try to look incognito while

wondering if they'll come because they love
the cocktails or to sell more gum.

BILL KUSHNER

My Love Life

I am intent on improving my love life
& to squeeze the receptacle end to release any
of the penis, as the sperm can be released
against the penis at the ring area of the testy
penis. Store penis at room temperature, please
& do not expose penis to the light for when light
hits the penis the penis may my goodness break dance for joy
which joy can increase the potential for breakage. Breakage
bad. Baaad. & then, pretty soon, Bub, comes the Spring
& with Spring comes, you know what I'm saying? Spring,
when a young man's heart & hand beats faster & ever ever
faster! Say, is this the Empire State Building I have my hairy hand
wrapped around, & are you King Kong? Well, well, hello there,
Mister Kong.

CLAUDIA LAROCCO

Just What He Wanted

The concierge is full of terrors

Errors in the pantry don't give him pause

But when she takes down her hair

When she opens that ruined-teeth maw and hisses her sex down the corridor

All the colors go go go

Little bluey, do that do-see-do. Oh, honey, not that.

She walk the best men

We send the rest them down the hole

So many places to stick that wand

Stirred, shaken. Distressed. We're nothing if we don't do a little pretend.

RONNA LEBO

À Bas le Robot

Sine qua non became both
bride and widow in the intro
an ass-kiss stereophonic switch
to happiness in the bladder

introducing ennui, mentioned
in an earlier episode Um Yeah
marked as spam between
le rest de la famille

applied to text mining gender
across *Digital Humans Quarterly*
another hand is determined
in a room smelling of Windex

to sell mediated politicians
comparative studies of women
in retail (morphology a threat
with centrist pitch) paranoid
of reverse invasion in the Louvre

a most popular contemporary giant
man falling hard for vulnerability
in full length trousers on a terrace atop
le Place D'Armes shops

nude in high quality format
How-To-Make-Euros-Go-Farther is likely
to get fast and filling contrast in le travail
but let's keep our minds and hearts
open to the other thing

MICHAEL LEONG

[untitled]

For Halloween, you were a playboy in pajamas
and I was a quivering bundle of synecdoches.

You were marooned behind a mask of Venetian red,
grazing on the synthetic grass of a putting green

while I was a disingenuously designed outlet mall,
your buxom biomorphic fantasy.

You: a Cheshire Cat at Mardis Gras.
Me: an ex-hand model, reengineered for maximum undulancy.

Always the gentleman, you plied me with orange
martinis and made a plush, Procrustean bed

just for me — I, your exquisite corpse, airbrushed,
collaged from old *Hustler* magazines.

At the night's end, I didn't bother to ash your cigarette,
we were so spent: even your fingers were in detumescence.

SHARON MESMER

I Am Cocked-Up with Over-Power

after Peter Saul's *Viva la Difference*

The God of the overpowering I AM is in ME!
now that I am cocked-up with over-power.

And it is the fiery I AM of poon pregret –
the signature position of the nigh-immortal
half elf/half octopus Bitch Queen of Hell –
that I am cocked-up with,
a cocked-up washer-woman of labial wings
finessing a finely tuned vajayjay cupcake
into a magpie-ish battle-stance that appeals to unicorns.
Each sentience of overpower seems
a cocked-up overpowering of the amateur radio rooster
who is also cocked-up with over-power,
and the perplexed logic of warlock action plans.

What gorgeous high elves you have, Sister Mooncow!
cocked-up with lollipops and six tits.
A rockin' cock-maid splays all the agility aspects
of the dark path of prairie venom,
which cocked-up overpower reveals to be merely
the dream of dividing the Escarole of Oneness
into fanny yogurt fairies and deep-house bears
who grow their own condoms and encode their own
bellicose gecko-loaders.

Unfortunately for you, Mooncow,
Pirate Baby's Cabana Battle Street Fight 2010
didn't have enough money in the budget
for an elfin Adolf Hitler sporting Henry Kissinger tits.
But in *Zombie Lust From Scotland*
the blood flows, teens die, breasts are exposed,
and a shit-ton of space-goats, blood elves and crack-rabbits
come out of nowhere screaming "SAVE THE GNOMES!"

That could've been you, Poo-fur Bootybot.
Expect a toy anal ATM soon.

TOM OBRZUT

Preparatory to a Fugue, Abattoir

Light a candle, incense; offer water

I dream about the hoboes
The wobblies
The Digger nation
Cartography
Helium balloons
And whiskey

A lucid dream
Walking around looking for
36 wise people who
Will save the world
Or burn it down
But I open my mouth, no sound

Harry told me he didn't
Know about hidden tsadikim
So I called for him on a cell phone
In a Night wet alley
He told me I should count rats
Not here, not London
I asked him how to go
He said think of it, you're there
I couldn't

Harry was always living on the street
By that he meant church steps
Where they let the missing lay
(They lie!)
Except for tonight

He really preferred East 52nd
A block full of boxes
Complaints from rich apartment dwellers
Friends from the city
New York's finest
New York's strongest
And a psychiatrist named Frank

Also erotic dreams
Of potato chips and sour cream
The whole tequila
Nachos and professional football on tv

Samsara looks like this
Red and brassy
Or as real as delusion
Never delivers what it never delivers
You want that?
Call Joe's pizza

Usually it's around Christmas
Watching all those miracles on 41st Street
The way Rudolf
A stag film on Bachelors night

Wait wait, I'll get it straight

Picture how much picture there is
Then take an unsatisfying feeling
Backlit with neon

It's a show you could fake to Vegas
Drink a bottle half full
The kind with some heavy percentage
Snort up a whole bunch of sensation
Let your life flash before your eyes

Start praying

THADDEUS RUTKOWSKI

In the Mood

Your black eyes light up when you see those pink and brown breasts with their multiple nipples. A grin breaks out across your face as you insert your finger in your partner's ear – if it is her ear and not her nose or mouth. It's hard to tell where her face is, beneath that curly hair. No matter; it's time for cocktails on the satin-covered bed. You've got your martini, and she's got what may be a daiquiri. Her glass is sitting in a suggestively hollow dimple. Bluebirds fly like clouds in formation. The sky is so close your shadow falls on it. A manicured lawn surrounds the bed, and the grass is a fine place to kneel.

One of the multiple nipples grazes your chin, reminding you of a kiss—a human kiss. But are these nipples and dimples human? Now that you think of it, your partner's species is questionable. The genitals look familiar, but the overall form is globular. You might have to pick up your cigarette and smoke on this. After a few puffs – and sips of your cocktail—you may be able to climb from the lawn to the bed and lie back on the satin pillows, content in the knowledge that it's the mood, not the taxonomy, that's important. You are grinning from ear to ear. She's squishing up against you. You're in the mood for (what do you call it?) love. Yes, that's what's in the air, along with the bird-shaped clouds.

CATHERINE SHAINBERG

Welcome to Ghiza Paradise Hotel

for you, my pink dolly gum
grape eyed Cleopatra, syrup of a girl
she no more bugaboo nose, her slippery cell
in chains, beguined, coagulated and moiled
just for you, friend

she straddles the croco bone and rib caged sandy shoe
It floats, an unsteady vulva of ethological behavior,
across the desert blue, seething
between pyramid tips and orchidaceous dusk

gurgling innocent, a hemorrhage all udder and tits
little vice made of sugar and spice and snips and snails
her *de capello* friends' furious scales enlaced
licks her finger to her purple, coos of coming attractions

virescent sibilants, triple swelling gardenia poison
I kill you with love

TARA SKURTU

Anomalies

after Peter Saul's *Viva la Difference*

I. Broken Heart Syndrome

I've been here before. Asleep
last night, dreamed myself awake

in a fluorescent, spot-lit recovery
room. Heart muscles malleable,

a mound of grey clay hanging
like loose electric wire bulging

from a precise   hole   in a wall.

II. Phantom Limb

one synapse   fired
                      at another
but   missed.
          A dam
                        broke
a lake filled   entire town

       submerged
fingers   first

in the wet   dark   my hand
                        slips
       inside
a familiar
         hole

III. Breast Augmentation

Two gauzed mounds, symmetric
                across my sternum, a corset
                                of cotton dressing, bound.

The doctor undresses my wounds,
                examines the saline spheres, satisfied
                                by the work of his craftsmanship.

In the mirror I discover my nipples
                replaced with tiny pink penises, erect.
                                He assures me, exactly what I
wanted.

SALLY VAN DOREN

Isn't She Beautiful

Two nipples protruding from brown skin.
Two nipples protruding from pink skin.
Two nipples protruding from yellow skin.
Four vaginas. Blond hair. Satin sheets.
No face. No butt.
One crazed red man with cigarette getting drunk.
Lots of green grass and blue sky.

PAUL VIOLI

Stalin and Mao Schtickomythia

What's what?

What's up?

What's up with you?

What's it look like?

What do you mean?

What do you mean what do I mean?

What's eating you?

What do you care?

What's your problem?

What's it to you?

What are you, a wiseguy?

What if I am?

What if I –

What if you what?

What are you, deaf?

What makes you ask?

What's this all about?

What's in it for me?

Whatever you say.

What a deal.

JOHN YAU

I Less Am You Let

after Peter Saul's *Viva la Difference* (2008)

In your
Sweetened

Dent
I praise

My pine-
Cone

Stem-
Ware

Now all
Flares

In your
Glove

You
Pour

Sweet
Swag

Slim
Shimmy

And
Shine

Inflatable
Star

Let your
Clover moon

Moan down
The chute

Nothing
A
Puffy
Dragon

Like me
Likes more

Than a pink
Teddy bear

Without
A face

To hang
On

SCOTT ZIEHER

Fatty

"Life does not need joy, but it needs more
common remedies against insensibility"

C.H. SISSON, CHRISTOPHER HOMM

Perforation – pulsing
Like a blue pimple.
These are fur-knuckle-berry
Shrimp-donkeys.
Bubbles dripping
Up.

Shit his pants
On the way to the taco
Standing stock still
Like a stupid statue
Made for the public
Pubis.

Triple va-jay-jay –
Silly man sticking
His stinking forehead
Forward like summer
Stuck, trickling.
Nothing

So sticky
As the velvet stench.

The pillow's a suite
Of sweet fingers
Distended from
An arm that isn't

So much a tentacle
As a stretch of broke
Up rat-pattern passage
Extenuations.
Language, my ass.
Morass, more ass.

Aren't you
Kidding me
With the biggest rot-fruit
Cigarette about to float
Away in a free martini.
Her drink is orange.

No brooding nipples.
No drooping rubes.
Naked not nude.
Your porous difference
Is good and gory.
Go away.

CONTRIBUTORS

SUSAN BERGER-JONES grew up in Pittsburgh, Pennsylvania and now lives in Brooklyn, New York. She is both an architect and a poet. Currently she is working on two chapbooks: a series of poems after the painter Francis Bacon with Judson Evans, and a series of drawings/poems with the painter Darcy Mann.

TODD COLBY has published four books of poetry: *Ripsnort* (1994), *Cush* (1995), *Riot in the Charm Factory: New and Selected Writings* (2000), and *Tremble & Shine* (2004), all published by Soft Skull Press. Todd has performed his poetry on PBS and MTV, and his collaborative books and paintings with artist David Lantow can be seen in the Brooklyn Museum of Art and The Museum of Modern Art special collections libraries. Todd serves on the Board of Directors for The Poetry Project, where he has also taught several poetry workshops, and he posts new work on gleefarm.blogspot.com.

LORRAINE DORAN holds a J.D. and a MFA in poetry from New York University. She has been the recipient of a grant from the Jerome Foundation, and an artist in residence at the Anderson Center for Interdisciplinary Studies. Currently, she teaches in the Expository Writing Program at NYU.

JUDSON EVANS is Director of Liberal Arts at The Boston Conservatory, where he teaches Ancient Greek culture and literature and a course on Utopian Communities. His work is represented in the third edition of Cor Van Den Heuvel's *The Haiku Anthology* (Norton, 1999), in the first English language anthology of haibun, edited by Bruce Ross: *Journeys to the Interior* (Tuttle, 1998) and in a chapbook *Mortal Coil,* from Leap Press. His poetic monologue *Scrabble Ridge* was staged as a performance piece by choreographer/dancer Julie Ince Thompson as part of the Fleet Boston Celebrity series in 2000. He was chosen as an "emerging poet" for the Association of American Poets by John Yau, and a selection of his poems with an essay on his work by John Yau appeared in *American Poet* in September of 2007.

JENNIFER HAYASHIDA is the translator of Fredrik Nyberg's *A Different Practice* (Ugly Duckling Presse, 2007) and Eva Sjödin's *Inner China* (Litmus Press, 2005). Recent projects have appeared in *Chicago Review, Harp & Altar,* and *Salt Hill,* and have also been included in art exhibitions domestically and abroad. She has received awards from the MacDowell Colony, the Lower Manhattan Cultural Council, the Jerome Foundation, and she was a 2009 New York Foundation for the Arts Fellow in Poetry. She recently completed a manuscript of poems entitled *A Machine Wrote This Song,* and is now at work on an autoethnographic essay, "The Autonomic System." She lives in Brooklyn, New York, where she is assistant fiction editor at *Fence* magazine and works as Acting Director of the Asian American Studies Program at Hunter College.

EILEEN B. HENNESSEY is a native of Long Island, and lives in New York City. Translator of foreign-language documentation, and adjunct associate professor of translation at New York University, her poems have been published in *Artful Dodge, Cream City Review, The Literary Review, Paris Review, Sanskrit,* and *Western Humanities Review.*

BONI JOI received a MFA in poetry from Columbia University, and has been nominated twice for a Pushcart Prize. Her poems have appeared in *Arbella, Boog City Reader, Long Shot, Lungfull, Ocular Press, Big Hammer, MaiNtENaNt3: a journal of contemporary dada writing & art* by Three Rooms Press, *The Brooklyn Rail* and many other journals. She has read her poetry at numerous venues in New York city and elsewhere.

BILL KUSHNER roams the streets of New York looking for Love and Poetry, and he just may find you!

CLAUDIA LA ROCCO's poems have appeared in such publications as *The Brooklyn Rail* and failbetter.com, and she reads regularly in New York City. Her collaborations with visual artists have been shown in High Desert Test sites 5 in Joshua Tree, California, Janet Kurnatowski Gallery in Greenpoint, Brooklyn, and the Kibbutz Gallery in Tel Aviv, Israel among others, and she is currently working on a project with Thomas Micchelli. She writes about dance for the *New York Times* and serves as cultural critic for WNYC New York Public radio. She is or has been a faculty member or guest lecturer in a variety of settings, including the MFA Art Criticism and Writing program at the School of Visual Arts, the NEA Arts Journalism Institute in Dance at the American dance Festival and the Springdance/festival in the Netherlands. She lives in Brooklyn.

RONNA LEBO received a MFA from Mason Gross School of the Arts, and currently teaches at Kean University. She performed for twelve years as Alice B. Talkless, won a Jackie 60 New Artist Award, and was included in two CMJ music festivals. In 2007 she received a New Jersey State Fellowship for the Arts. Her poetry has been published in *Ocular Press*, *Arbella*, *Long Shot*, *Big Hammer*, *Words*, *This Broken Shore*, *Whim Wit*, and the anthology *Will Work for Peace*, edited by Brett Axel.

MICHAEL LEONG's poetry career began in the sixth grade when he won his first and only poetry prize in Mr. Harrison's class for a haiku about a snake. Since then, he has received degrees in English and Creative Writing from Dartmouth College, Sarah Lawrence College, and Rutgers University and has published poems in journals such as *Bird Dog*, *jubilat*, *Marginalia*, *Opium Magazine*, *Pindeldyboz*, and *Tin House*. He is the author of *I, the Worst of All* (blazeVOX [books], 2009), a translation of the Chilean poet Estela Lamat, and *e.s.p.* (Silenced Press, 2009), a collection of poetry. Visit him at michaelleong.wordpress.com and bigother.com.

SHARON MESMER is the author of the poetry collections A*nnoying Diabetic Bitch* (Combo Books, 2008), *The Virgin Formica* (Hanging Loose Press, 2008), *Vertigo Seeks Affinities* (Belladonna Books, 2006), *Half Angel, Half Lunch* (Hard Press 1998) and *Crossing Second Avenue* (ABJ Books, Japan, 1997). Fiction collections are *The Empty Quarter* (Hanging Loose, 2000), *Ma Vie a Yonago* (Hachette Litteratures, France, in French translation, 2006) and *In Ordinary Time* (Hanging Loose Press, 2005). Her blog is http://virginformica.blogspot.com/ .

TOM OBRZUT has been the editor of *Arbella Magazine* since 1987. He has read extensively in the New York metropolitan region and has been published by many small press magazines and web-sites. Tom uses both narrative and experimental styles in his work, but is interested primarily in documenting his work with street homeless and mentally ill people and in teaching the pleasures of poetry to those groups. *Arbella* and Tom's work with the homeless are archived by the State University of New York, Buffalo. Tom has also written a novel on his experiences with homeless people.

THADDEUS RUTKOWSKI is the author of the novels *Tetched* and *Roughhouse*. Both books were finalists for an Asian American Literary Award. He teaches fiction writing at the Writer's Voice of the West Side YMCA in Manhattan and is the fiction editor of *Many Mountains Moving*, a Colorado-based journal.

CATHERINE SHAINBERG has a MFA in poetry from New York University. She founded The School of Images, a Kabbalah school to advance awareness of imagination as a tool for healing and crea-tivity. Her book *Kabbalah and the Power of Dreaming* was published in 2005. Her next book *DreamBirth* is forthcoming. She has been published in *More Poems,* Alan Dugan's Poetry Workshops series, and Guggenheim Public. She has been a member of the writer's group, Off the Park, lead by John Yau, for the last five years.

TARA SKURTU is in the Creative Writing Honors program at the University of Massachusetts, Boston. In 2008 she was awarded an Honorable Mention by Elizabeth Alexander for UMB's Academy of

American Poets Prize. She represented UMB at the Massachusetts Poetry Festival in 2009. She has been a featured poet in venues around the Boston area. This is her first published work.

SALLY VAN DOREN's collection of poems, *Sex at Noon Taxes* (Louisiana State University Press), won the 2007 Walt Whitman award from the Academy of American Poets. Her poems appeared recently in: *American Poet, Barrow Street, Boulevard, 5AM, Margie, The New Republic, River Styx, Southwest Review, 2River* and *Verse Daily*. She lives in St. Louis, Missouri and Cornwall, Connecticut.

PAUL VIOLI's most recent book, his eleventh, is *Overnight*, from Hanging Loose Press. His other books are *Fracas, The Curious Builder*, and *Likewise*, from Hanging Loose Press, and a selection of his longer poems, *Breakers*, from Coffee House Press. He teaches at Columbia University and the New School graduate writing program.

JOHN YAU has published books of poetry, fiction, and criticism. Among the poetry books are *Paradiso Diaspora, Ingrish* (a collaboration with Thomas Nozkowski), *Borrowed Love Poems, Forbidden Entries, Berlin Diptychon, Edificio Sayonara* and *Corpse and Mirror*, a National Poetry Series book selected by John Ashbery. He has been Arts editor of *The Brooklyn Rail* since March 2004, and the co-publisher of Black Square Editions/Brooklyn Rail Books. He is an Associate Professor at Mason Gross School of the Arts, Rutgers University, the State University of New Jersey. Yau lives in New York City.

SCOTT ZIEHER is the author of two books of poetry, *Virga* (2005) and *Impatience* (2009), both published by Emergency Press, and a book of found photography, *Band of Bikers* (powerHouse books, 2010). His poems have appeared in *The Believer, The Iowa Review, Jubilat* and *The Siennese Shredder.* He lives and works in New York City with his wife, Andrea. They are the co-owners of ZieherSmith, a contemporary art gallery established in 2003.